THIS BOOK BELONGS TO:

_____

We hope you enjoy this book and would love to see your work! Tag us with a pic of your creations on Instagram @HollandReidColoring and for more inspired coloring books, check out Holland Reid's other publications on Amazon.

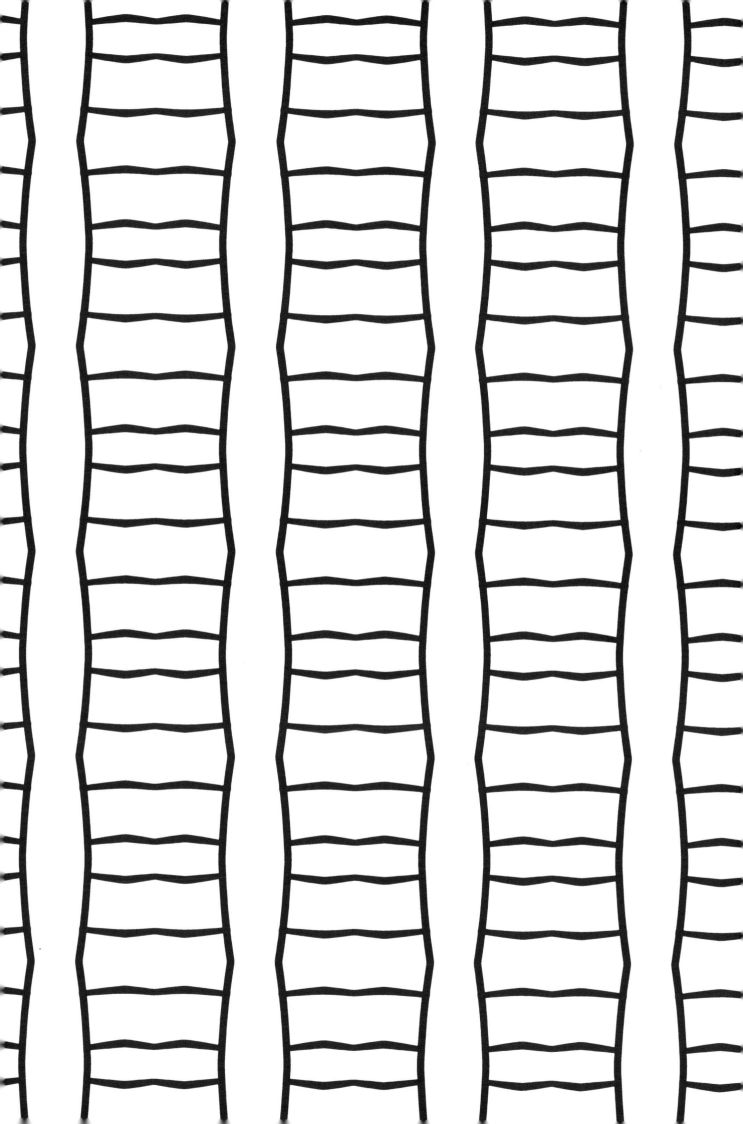

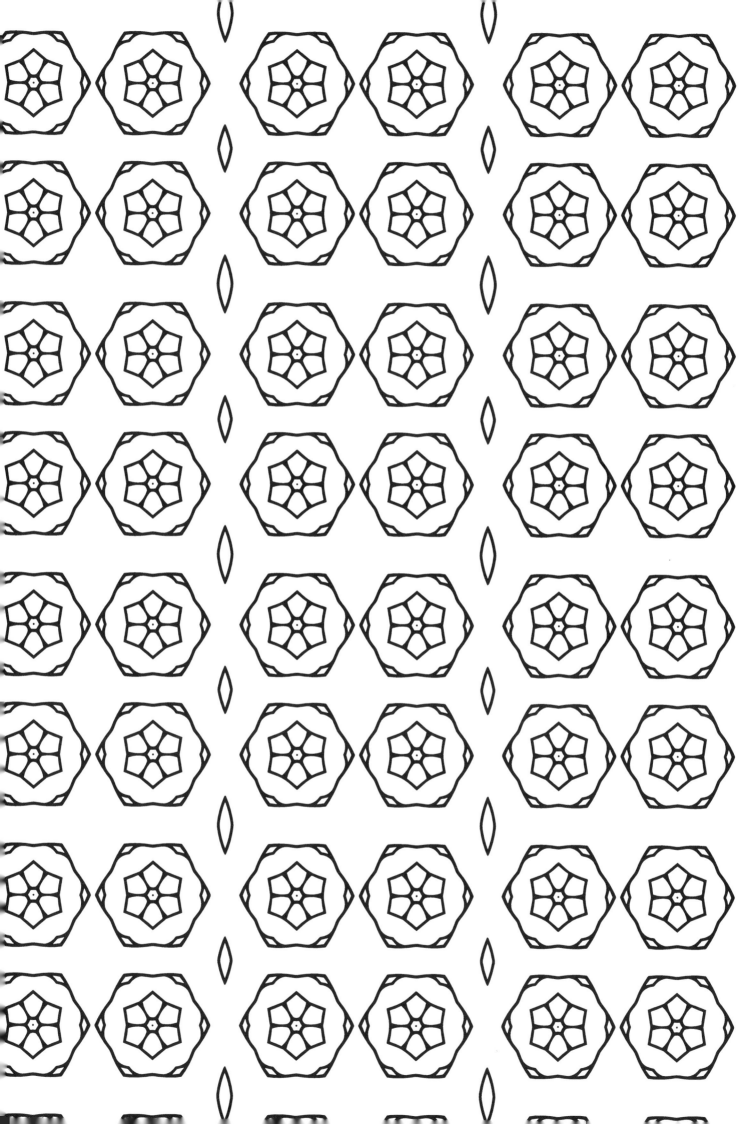

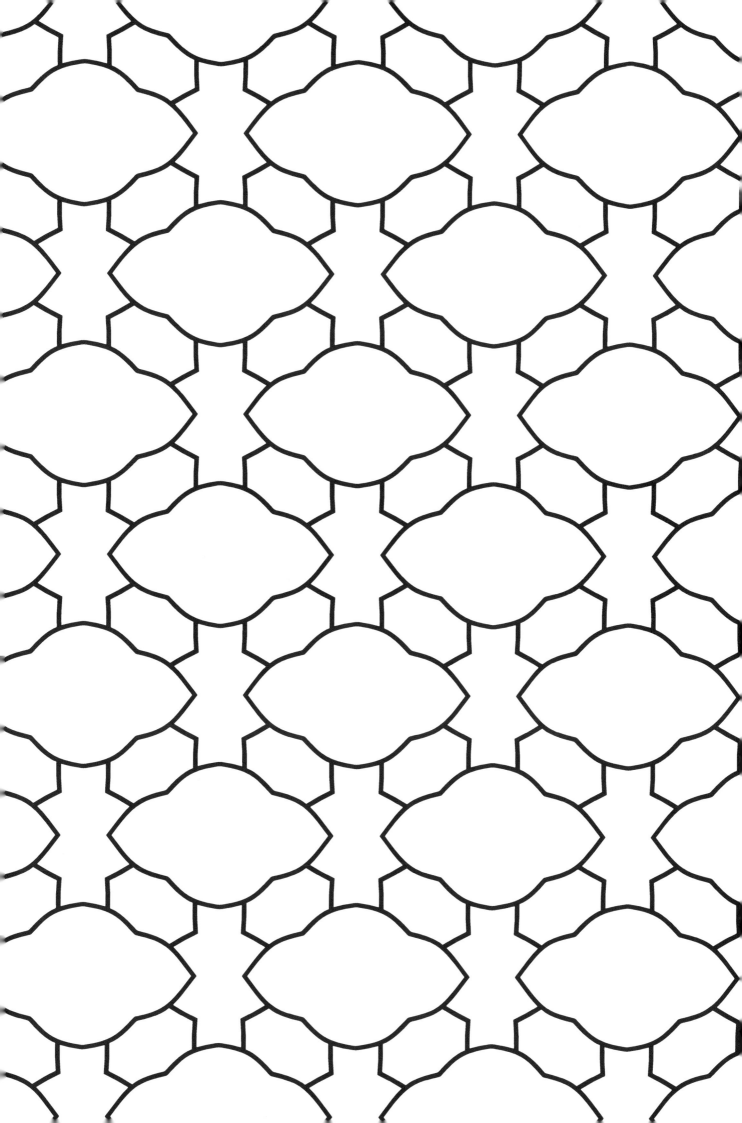

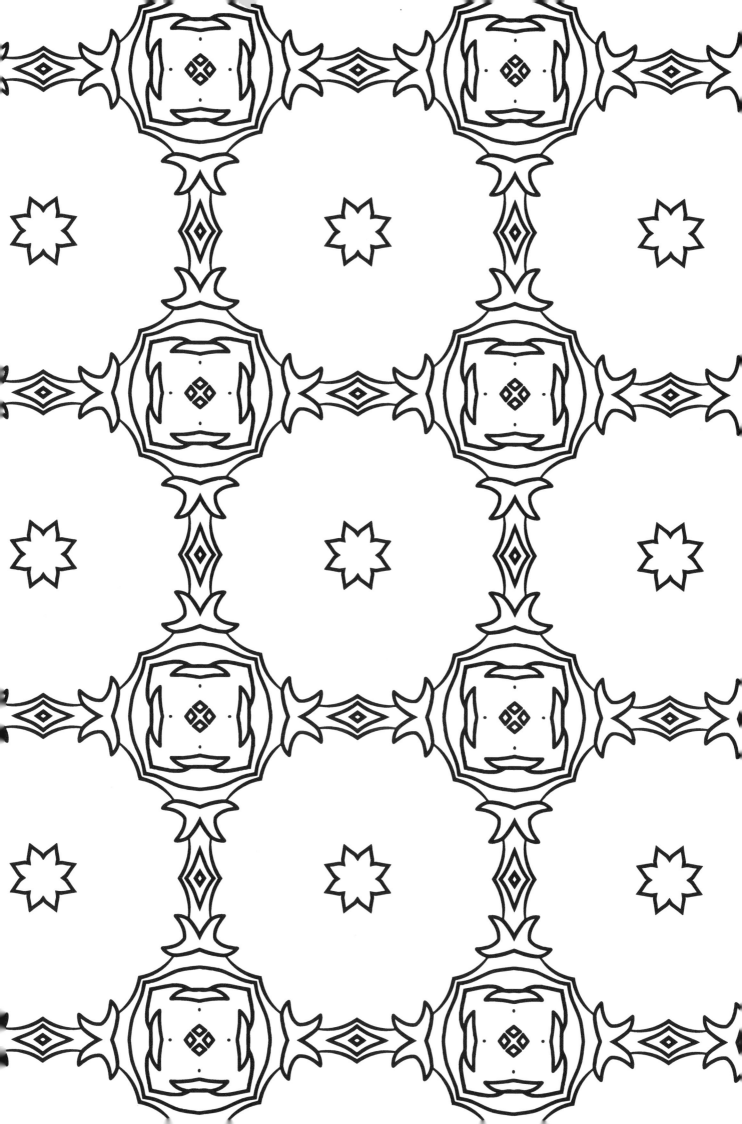

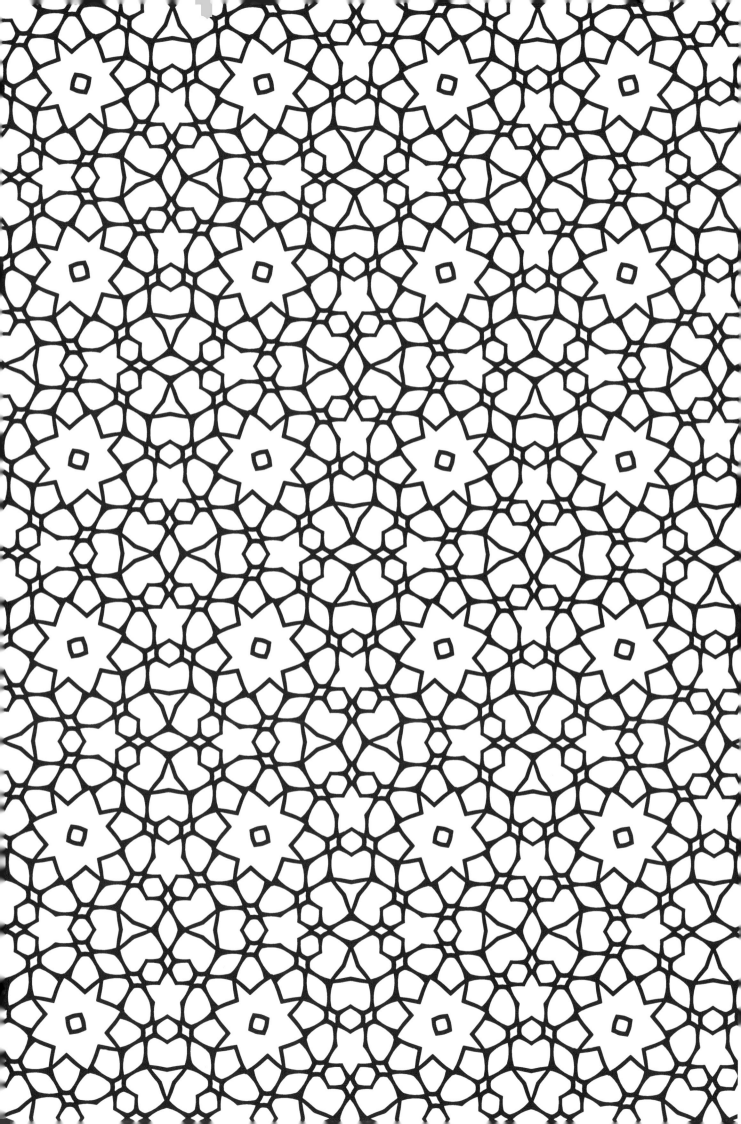

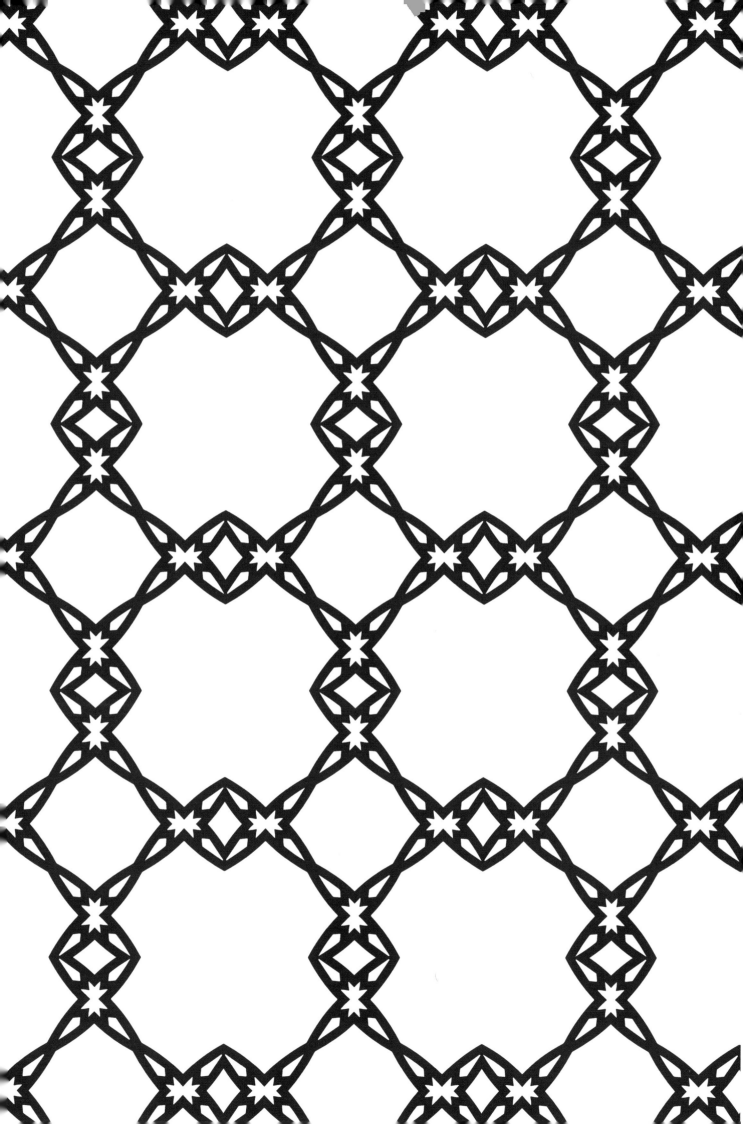

Made in the USA
Coppell, TX
11 October 2024

38502439R00068